DOWN SOUTH
Homes and Interiors in South Africa

Paul Duncan

Photographs Fritz von der Schulenburg

Jonathan Ball Publishers

DOWN SOUTH
Homes and Interiors in South Africa

First published in 2004 by Jonathan Ball Publishers (Pty) ltd
PO Box 33977 Jeppestown 2043

2 4 6 8 10 9 7 5 3 1

Publisher Dick Wilkins
Designer Rob House
Editor Mary Armour

Reproduction by Unifoto (Pty) Ltd, Cape Town
Printed by Tien Wah Press (Pte) Ltd, Singapore

ISBN 1 868 421 961

Contents

Bold New World

DOWN SOUTH: Homes and Interiors in South Africa features a South African decor finally come of age. In May 1998 the first issue of *Condé Nast House & Garden* was published in South Africa, with myself as editor and featuring interiors photographed by, among others, Fritz von der Schulenburg. This internationally acclaimed photographer first made his name with the launch of *The World of Interiors*, has worked for publications that include *Vogue* and *Architectural Digest* as well as both the British and American House & Garden magazines. This will be the first book featuring Fritz von der Schulenburg's work to be published in South Africa. And it is the first book to feature such a diverse range of South African homes.

Much of the excitement and vitality evident in decor circles and amongst readers of *Condé Nast House & Garden* has been due not only to Fritz's brilliant photography, but also to the variety of homes chosen and combined with great flair and panache. Most of us had no idea how much talent, energy and style was out there until we saw it in the magazine. The timing was propitious, as the country moved out of social and cultural isolation: returning artists, architects and decorators brought in global influences, interpreted in a local idiom, and local craftsmen, decorators and artists were discovered by the international 'talent scouts' of the decor industry. Within recent years many South African decorators have become highly sought-after worldwide and the increasing popularity of the country's annual Rooms on View decor exhibition is a definite indication that the local decor industry is coming into its own. Homemakers around South Africa now have more choices and opportunities than ever before to develop and express their personal style in their interiors.

This isn't a book exclusively about the 'decorated' interior – although some of the places featured illustrate the work of leaders in the field – like Stephen Falcke, Ralph Krall, Graham Viney, Julia Twigg, Boyd Ferguson and Nthabi Taukobong. The work of most of the decorators featured is internationally known: Stephen Falcke is a past winner of the Andrew Martin International Designer of the Year Award (2000), and Graham Viney was voted by *Architectural Digest* in the United States as one of the world's 100 top decorators. It is about the lifestyles that inform choices to do with architecture, landscaping, entertaining and relaxed living.

The range and diversity of contemporary South African homes and interiors is extraordinary. Whether in the bush, in the city, by the sea, or in the desert, they're places that stand out because of their owners' dedication to the art of living comfortably, stylishly and appropriately in this new world. Some places are decorated, others aren't. Most have a spontaneous ebullience and are larger than life. Still others have been carefully stage-managed by homemakers who enjoy the unconventional use of conventional things. Even game lodges and hotels are designed and decorated to express individual style. The old guard has moved on, and what no longer works has to go. This is a bold new world and South Africans aren't afraid of rocking the boat or shooting a few sacred cows.

These are the kinds of places you'd expect to find in *Condé Nast House & Garden*. While the houses featured are representative of South Africa's diverse choices and approaches, this is not intended to be a comprehensive, 'last word' on local interiors. There's a great deal more out there, with new architectural styles and decor emerging all the time. And anyway it is too soon to claim that most South Africans get to exercise personal choice in where and how they live. It seems insensitive to dwell on 'shack decor,' since all too often in South Africa's history, harsher circumstances – war, floods, drought, apartheid, poverty – have dictated where and how people lived. As the African-American writer James Baldwin commented: 'Perhaps home is not a place/ but simply an irrevocable condition.'

Is there an all-South African interior style, the way there's an all-English one, or an all-French one? Distinctively South African styles are emerging. Think of local style as a loose amalgam of different things. What makes it different is originality. Borrowing bits and pieces from elsewhere is acceptable. Slavish imitation is not. None of the creators of the houses published here ever loses a sense of milieu. And the raw decorative materials available have no equal. In fact South Africa is such an attractive commodity at the moment that traditional and contemporary arts and crafts, cultural artefacts, the products of artisans' workshops and the textile and ceramic studios are regularly plundered from abroad. London-based decorator Gabhan O'Keeffe, a regular visitor, says, 'things that are over-familiar to South Africans seem exotic in Europe.'

We've been set apart by the remoteness of our location. Our political status for the greater part of the 20th century didn't help either. Shut away for so long in the sun at the bottom of the world, South Africans looked inwards. Not altogether a bad thing – while there's no denying we stagnated culturally, something intensely homegrown emerged from our diverse traditions and is now reaching maturity. Out there everybody wants it.

In South Africa we don't have the grandiose 19th-century apartment buildings with enfilades of rooms you'd find in Paris or New York, or terraces of tall stucco houses with a staircase up the middle and a fireplace on every floor like you see in London. This is a newer country with few noteworthy old domestic structures. All too often we've succumbed to architectural pastiche, but the really good stuff has lasted well. What we do have though is plenty of space for new houses designed organically to maximise, say, a spectacular view. We can fulfil our dreams when it comes to building a new home. That's one of our greatest luxuries and it has given rise to some spectacular modern domestic architecture. This book has a sampling of it – the Tree House (Van der Merwe Miszewski), Casa Westcliff (Silvio Rech and Lesley Carstens), Beach House (Stefan Antoni Architects) and Karooltjie (Etienne Bruwer) to name just a few of those that made it onto these pages.

The South African interior gets its particular zest from the informal way we live. The starting point of good decorating is whether or not an interior is comfortable and user-friendly. If it's not, what's the point of it? Most interiors featured here happily ignore any distinctions between formal and informal. In contemporary South Africa there are no rigid period styles to contend with, few social hierarchies that dictate styles of living or entertaining and even fewer inherited styles of building that prevent ease of communication between areas of the house. And it's a fact of life here that for every hard chair there's almost certainly a couple of easy ones, for every indoor reception room there's almost certainly a shady stoep or two. Anything goes, as long as it's done with panache and style.

Gail Behr's house at Newlands Farm near Plettenberg Bay is a prime example. There is a pizza oven facing the fireplace in the dining room which, separated from the kitchen by an Edwardian-style 'shop counter', is where guests are encouraged to have drinks. A living room doesn't exist, if you discount the series of anterooms culminating in a well-upholstered stoep. Artefacts on show are not family heirlooms and precious ornaments but ranks of serious cooking equipment. These, not the silver teapots, get the Silvo treatment. On shelves built specially to hold them are stacks of chunky, mismatched, white-only crockery displayed as though it was the family porcelain. This is fresh, new and unexpected.

Managing her house like a stage set, Behr has set up individual tableaux all over her place for conversation, and sofas and armchairs are arranged accordingly and invitingly. In a house that grows organically in an ad hoc manner, beds and tables are constructed by the carpenter to fit outlandish spaces, walls are knocked through to reveal a fresh view, or sealed up when a view's become boring. Concrete staircases are left uncarpeted and windows remain unglazed. It's a do-whatever-you-like interior with fans for the summer and under-floor heating for the winter, even outside on the stoep. And where others might have cows grazing in their farm pastures, here there are giraffe and rhino. Anarchy reigns.

Parkside, Ralph Krall's house in Cape Town, also has unexpected elements. Krall's bedroom is itself a reception room reminiscent of those bedrooms used by Louis XV for his morning levées in public. Guests perch on the edge of a four-poster in a room lined with books and pictures, with a view through open doors to the courtyard beyond with its pots of topiary and carpeted flagstones. It's original. At Royal Malewane, Liz Biden and Krall put most of the furniture

outside in the open, on the raised deck which is all that separates you from the wildlife. How thrilling to sit in a nimbus of lamp light in a slip-covered armchair on a carpeted deck under the stars and listen to wild animals coughing in the bush a few feet away.

At Karel Nel's Gauteng home the rooms have been curated for a more austere and cerebral purpose. An important collection of African artefacts is housed in vast storage areas and certain items are brought out to be strategically placed and observed. In a house without a kitchen, the sitting room – a huge, barrel-vaulted bunker designed by two bridge engineers – doubles as a painting studio. In one room there's a large *coco de mer* branch. For two years now Nel has been working on a commission for North Island Lodge in the Seychelles, in a series he has entitled *Elegies to the Forest*. For now he's surrounding himself with rare plant materials he's transforming into art. 'The *coco de mer* is only found on Pralin in the Seychelles and has the largest leaves in the world,' says Nel. He lives amidst the raw materials of his art. 'For me there is no separation between art and life.'

Karen Roos, at her 18th-century Cape Dutch farmstead in the city, finds that the spaces she inhabits are best treated as blank canvases. She has created new dynamics of scale, balance and ultimately surprise resulting in a total lack of formal cohesion. 'I purposefully steered clear of the sacred cows of the Cape Dutch decor vernacular, like armoires and copper chandeliers,' she says. In her home, she's the curator whose 'rule-breaking instincts for composition and understatement have flushed new charm into the traditional,' says writer Diana Vives. Breaking the rules is never as much fun as when it's utterly unexpected.

At Long Barn, European antiques sit not on polished wooden floors or hand-woven rugs but mostly on rustic hemp carpeting the floors from wall to wall. If this could speak it would play the trollop to the blue-blooded antiques that stand on it. The owner of the house exchanged her stately former home for this one in an effort to pursue a more relaxed, informal lifestyle. Decorator Julia Twigg, whose style is simple and unfussy anyway, hit the note appropriately – even in the drawing room a grand, glass-fronted Cape armoire filled with delicate Minton porcelain is paired with a group of rough, chubby Provençal pots. There's a deliberate move away from the expected and the precious.

From the informal to the primitive, Casa Westcliff, also in Johannesburg, is the most dramatic exercise yet in making the unusual seem utterly conventional. Designed by Silvio Rech and Lesley Carstens, it is essentially a series of mud huts crowning the summit of a hillock in the middle of the city. It's 21st-century Rider Haggard. Not only are its simple shapes reminiscent of African tribal vernacular, but it's a rough-cast, beautiful building with womb-like spaces and intricate ornamental detail and pattern. I suspect that this evokes most nearly the mythic Africa of many people's imaginations.

Leadwood Lodge in the KwaZulu-Natal countryside has the same energy, echoing through its stony bulk the ancient Zimbabwe ruins. There's a fantastical edge which just stops short of parodying a set in a Hollywood epic. At Karooltjie in Barrydale, there's a similar typology (although the roofs are composed with dry stone from the region and not thatch), and these buildings – Karooltjie, Leadwood Lodge and Casa Westcliff – in their form and planning, preclude any lifestyle not completely informal and completely at home in Africa.

Informality is synonymous with ease. Gauteng decorator Stephen Falcke's garden house in Parktown North, Johannesburg, is only for play. It's the modern local equivalent of Marie Antoinette's dairy. He doesn't live there – in the sense that it's not where he returns each evening after work, where he wakes in the morning, does his accounts or keeps his laundry. It's a place purely for relaxation. There are no bedrooms and there's neither ironing board nor television. He goes there to swim, garden, read, have dinners with friends and then, when he's had enough, he just closes the door and goes home. You couldn't get more laid back.

At Beach House at Cape Agulhas, designed in conjunction with the owner by Mark Rielly of Stefan Antoni Architects, you enter the house through sliding glass panels into a single large space housing kitchen, dining and sitting areas, in its entirety dominated at one end by a huge fireplace and at the other by an island kitchen counter. It's open plan, but deconstructed to the extent that the visitor feels he's climbed in through a window rather than the front door. Your sense of arrival is skewed. It's a social leveller designed to put everybody who enters at ease.

This, then, is a book about lived-in, livable spaces got up in a variety of guises. What we choose to surround ourselves with says a great deal about our preferred realities. At the Tree House, in Gianna Ghersi's living room a Norman Foster steel-and-glass dining table that looks like a lunar landing craft shares the same space as long beautiful Onda sofas by Saporiti with their leather upholstery and steel supports. Uncompromisingly modern, nothing could be more appropriate in a building whose architects, Anya and Macio Miszewski, are always striving to achieve a balance between poetic narrative and the rational. Vast windows let in the surrounding woodland and there are views up towards the summit of Table Mountain and down to the stream running through the garden on its way to the sea.

At Villa Libert in St James, a Spanish Colonial landmark of the False Bay coastline, Keith Skeel resorts to the unexpected as a way of filling the gaps. The uptight Edwardian panelled sitting room downstairs is livened up with carved African stools, grotesque tribal totems blackened with age, and abstract stone sculptures from Zimbabwe, juxtaposed with big, shapeless slip-covered armchairs and sofas. It's the Hampshire rectory come to the seaside in Africa. It's also a shot-in-the-arm for a prim room not that well-suited to beachside living. The architect, it would seem, didn't have a clue, which is why Skeel opened up a range of grim little rooms upstairs and let in the light and the magnificent sea views. On the chest by the door in the sitting room there's also the skull of a hippo whose provenance is not as peculiar as the skull in the passage at Kersefontein. The former came from an antique shop in Kalk Bay. Its Kersefontein cousin, on the other hand, was the last hippo to have lived on the Berg River up the West Coast, and was shot by Martin Melck in 1867. There's a nasty hole in the skull to prove it.

Craig Kaplan's Victorian house at Cheviot Place is certainly not a decorated house. Kaplan opened up a poky dwelling at the end of a terrace to create what's possibly the largest one-bedroom house in Cape Town. Both upstairs and down, suites of rooms are now only separated from one another by a fireplace, the walls on either side of the chimney breast having been removed to allow views into the spaces on either side and beyond. The place is filled from years of booty hunting in salesrooms and antique shops in Cape Town and Johannesburg. Simply things that have appealed to him over the years, many of them aren't supposed to work together. That they do is a happy coincidence.

Villa 16 in Sandhurst is a showcase for the work of South African craftsmen, put together by a globetrotting businessman who combines a sense of fun with a serious passion for collecting. Paris-based designer Serge Robin and South African architect Peter Hoffe were given creative carte blanche, the former designing everything from sofas and tables to curtains and carpeting, most of it manufactured in South Africa. 'The owner,' says writer Josef Talotta, 'is more than enthusiastic about South African craftsmanship,' calling it 'fantastic and incredible', and comparing it to the best in the world. The house also showcases the work of South African artists like André Naude, Tony Nkotsi, Simon Stone and Louis van Heerden. Master potter Hylton Nel's house in Calitzdorp also takes its hat off to the art of South Africa – in this case his own. But whereas

the owner of Villa 16 keeps his pieces in gallery-like order, Nel, the 'artist potter', puts his own irreverent whimsical ceramics to everyday use. Decorative jugs, bowls and pots by other artists surround him and serve as reference points and inspiration, but he likes to point out that he also has them there to eat off, to fill with wild flowers or to keep things in. They're practical in a house that has the same hardworking down-to-earth feel.

Informality and individuality are just two traits of the South African style. Another is the remarkable sense of place that seems to underpin the character of many Houses. Most respond magnificently to their location. One or two find themselves in the middle of inhospitable terrain that challenges their inhabitants to live comfortably. In defiance of this, the builders of 18th-century Kersefontein, for example, a Cape Dutch farmhouse marooned in the hot, dusty Sandveld on the West Coast, built a fine homestead using humble materials – like indigenous fruitwood, mud, thatch and reeds – that came easily to hand. And yet like many other Cape Dutch homesteads, according to Hans Fransen (*The Old Buildings of the Cape*, with co-author Mary Cook), 'its placement in the landscape transcends the limitations imposed by the materials and available technology and achieved results far beyond the sum of their parts.'

That was then. Nowadays houses, like Vygekraal, with its views over the rocky coastline near Plettenberg Bay, celebrate the drama of location. Unlike Vygekraal, which deliberately manipulates the natural drama, the castle at Knoetzie near Knysna is as picturesque as the setting. It clambers up the cliffs facing a cove, and has the rambling, organic quality of an edifice built over centuries. Built using local stone, it 'belongs' to this place – in much the same way as Kersefontein does. Little 19th-century Meer Rivier is no different, and was built with whatever came to hand in the nearby veld. Small windows and thick walls keep the cool in and the heat out in the summer, the opposite in the winter. Façades have been softened by lime washing and the building has a weathered and textured quality, a human scale of construction.

Back at Cape Agulhas, there's great sensitivity in the way that Beach House has been designed to address its site. You don't glimpse the house until you stumble on it as you approach over a low rise in front of it. The proximity of the sea is inescapable. Crayfish are caught in the rock pools below, the vast windows are open all day so that you can hear the sea and feel and smell the wind coming off it, while the colours of the building's materials mimic the rocks and grey skies on a stormy Cape afternoon. Tree House has a similarly intimate relationship to its setting. Not only do tall columns rising up through three storeys support the roof via a series of arms which echo the top branches of the tall pines surrounding the building, but sheer glass walls let the outdoors in.

Perhaps what sets apart all the houses in this book is the special dialogue between interiors and the outdoors. You'd have thought this would be a given the world over, but it's not. It helps here that the weather permits an easy relationship between the two. This is the essence of good living in South Africa. If you can't get it right – and all the houses in this book do – then you'd be missing the whole point of living in South Africa.

DOWN SOUTH, then, is a publication that hopefully will challenge our tired assumptions about the way we used to live and what might be possible in the future. The choice of interiors should intrigue anyone interested in how we live now in this country. To glimpse how others live well, albeit differently, is always irresistible. We've kept the text brief, informative and readable: the book as a whole is intended to encourage you as reader find your own decorating style. It will challenge, even infuriate, as well as inspire. But it is a book above all to enjoy.

PAUL DUNCAN

Tree House, Higgovale

'I built a house here because we wanted to live among the trees and we wanted to be able to see the trees through the glass – as if we were sitting in the middle of a forest,' says owner Gianna Ghersi. The resulting Tree House, designed by Anya and Macio Miszewski, is a masterpiece of contemporary architecture. It sits in a wooded valley below Table Mountain and in the shadow of Lion's Head. It is a diaphanous steel and glass structure that at night glows among the shadows of the giant stone pines that surround it. Not only can the owners see the pines through walls of glass but, within, five 'tree' columns rise from the ground and soar through three stories to the roof, which they support in a fan of five clusters of 'branches'. Inside, an undulating wall bisects the building from top to bottom and, cantilevered off it, on the top level is the reception room; below which is a middle level housing the bedroom and bathroom and, below that, on the ground floor, a guest suite and sitting room. The ground level is a solid, slate-clad base, while the two upper floors are nearly transparent. As the building rises upwards, it seems to dematerialise into almost nothing as it reaches for the sky.

Previous: *The living area is a lofty glazed box supported on high by fanned out beams on tall columns echoing the pines on the outside. The structure is delicate, the colours muted; this is a space that changes with the mood of the seasons and the time of day. Beyond the sofa in the background is a small terrace from which a spiral stair leads to the rooftop viewing platform.* Top: *The living area is itself a platform cantilevered from a serpentine wall cutting through the house from the lower ground level.* Below and opposite: *Furniture and fittings have been kept to a minimum, clean-lined and simple.*

Casa Westcliff, Johannesburg

This is the African-inspired house of most people's imaginations. Like something gleaned from the outer edges of Rider Haggard's texts, it transcends ethnic clichés to create something seemingly ancient and yet very contemporary. Although located in urban Johannesburg, it's been conceived as if it was a mountaintop village, with kitchen, dining room and living rooms each divided into a self-contained *khaya* and linked through a series of wooden decks and stone terraces. It is on a hill, however, surrounded by woods: its design, by Silvio Rech and Lesley Carstens, was influenced by the site. In many ways it's the physical manifestation of that most earthly of idylls – how great to live under a pigmented plaster dome the colour of the Westcliff soil, with polished cement underfoot and a range of textures surrounding you which are more usually found in the raw bush. And it's been put together 'with lots of collected bits from all around the world, particularly from African and island cultures, along with some architectural prototypes'. Adds architect Silvio Rech: 'You could never do this in Europe,' alluding to the fact that much of the home's architectural detail and furniture was built by hand on site by dedicated craftspeople who thrived on reinterpreting traditional skills with modern application.

Top: A totemic carved wooden bird stands sentinel at the entrance.
Right: In the dressing room study, the white coffee table designed by architect Silvio Rech is enhanced by the earthy colours all around it.

Above: *This might be architecture in touch with its roots, but the owners still need somewhere to swim in the summer.*
Design here is practical as well as aesthetic. **Right:** *Small but functional, the rustic kitchen is self-contained and warm in spirit.*

Above: *Wall-built banquettes in the bedroom. Before the project grew to more ambitious dimensions, this room was designed as a one-bedroomed mountaintop cottage.*

Right: *The extensive use of wood, pigmented plaster and polished cement, while creating continuity and tactility, also helps maintain a sense of locale and cultural context.*

Moray Place, Oranjezicht

Above: *In the main bedroom a headboard has been detailed with a pattern of porcupine quills.* **Right:** *In the den are lithograph prints by South African artist and photographer Stephen Inggs.*

The Cape Town city bowl home of Trevor Dykman, owner of African Light & Trading, has a racy and irreverent edge. It is in many ways an experimental laboratory to 'test-drive' new looks and products, always evolving and very much a work-in-progress. Right now, Dykman has relinquished his former neo-colonial look, and brought in a new decorative scheme that's altogether 'sexier and edgier' with Art Deco references in a startling colour palette of deep purple, cappuccino and off-white. His century-old double-storey Victorian terraced house has taken this updated look in its stride: the Venetian glass mirror and embossed leather console on scissor-legs in the entrance hall for example, lend a subtle sheen and glamour. It's the movie-star *manqué* in Trevor that's giving vent to a whole world of possibilities, one in which style and substance are as important as comfort and glamour.

Previous: *Dining-room walls are upholstered in a cappuccino stripe. Wall-mounted lighting features porcupine-quill lampshades.* Clockwise from top left: *A guest bedroom; the court-yard dining table; view from the landing; the bar area.* Right: *In the entrance hall a Venetian-style mirror and console of embossed leather are evidence of the owner's stock in trade.*

24

House Gevisser, Plettenberg Bay

Top left: *Mexican three-tiered chandelier with a splash of magenta colour.* Top right: *Multicoloured wicker chairs and ornate wall decoration give the dining terrace festive appeal.* Opposite: *A view of the house from the beach.* Overleaf left: *View into the main bedroom with watermelon-pink headboard and vibrant throws.* Overleaf right: *A simple colour scheme – blue, pink and white – is articulated mostly through the room's accessories. Washed by the sun all day long, this room's tempo is invigorating.*

'When it comes to beach life, I can't think of a better place in all the world,' says the owner of this beachfront home designed by architect Menno Meinesz, the master of the holiday home, built to make life as easy-going as possible. Although it's a big place that accommodates up to 10 adults staying at any one time, it's capable of shutting down so that only the main suite tucked away above the living area is in operation as a self-contained unit. White walls outside, and white walls and terracotta floors within: this is an appropriately neutral base from which to launch a jaunty decorating scheme where accents are blue and watermelon-pink. With four subsidiary bedroom suites and quirky little patios and terraces to fill, furnishings have been sourced mostly locally. But there are also Mexican rugs and blankets, Mexican glass and wrought-iron, together with seagrass mats, Pierre Frey fabrics, and other items come from Jos Graham in London and Stephen Falcke in Johannesburg. The result is an upbeat beach house that doesn't mind wet bottoms on sofas and sandy footprints on the floor. It's considered, well-planned and induces an instant and relaxed holiday tempo that's remarkably difficult to quit.

Kersefontein, Hopefield

Although the landscape around Kersefontein may not be as grandiloquent as you might expect the setting of a Cape Dutch homestead to be, its isolation nonetheless inspires a certain awe. Kersefontein lies behind the Piketberg, in the heart of the Sandveld, on the banks of the Berg River. That the house, built in the 18th century, has survived subsequent alterations virtually intact, is remarkable. Here lives Julian Melck, 'farmer, pig-killer, aviator' and organist at the local church in Hopefield, a descendant of the Martin Melck who bought the property in 1770. Generations of family furniture, much of it early Cape and of museum quality, fill the rooms. While certain pieces have always been there, over the years as fashions changed or things got damaged, certain pieces found their way into the attics and outbuildings where they lay mouldering until decorator Graham Viney retrieved them, had them repaired and put them into rooms he'd restored and redecorated. In making sense of historic Kersefontein for 21st-century living, Viney has helped bring it back to life. Kersefontein is still a working farm, but it's a curiosity as well, one much appreciated by paying guests who come to stay in the restored outbuildings amongst the pepper trees and bluegums lining the old werf behind the homestead.

Clockwise from top left: *The walls of a long passage that bisects the house are hung with hunting trophies and in the foreground is the skull of the last hippo seen on the Berg River; the late-Georgian colour scheme of the dining room was suggested by a watercolour circa 1835 of a remarkably similar room. The stamped wool damask for the curtains was specially woven in Yorkshire. The equestrian paintings recall the farm's days as the Cape's premier stud; old furniture has been gallantly renovated and recycled in the bedrooms.*

Left: *A bedroom with its brass bed dressed with yards of seersucker and its sweet-pea wallpaper, was at one time the farm's old dop room.* Right, above: *A sitting room has been furnished with interesting things rescued from decay in old store rooms and attics. Nothing went to waste. Nothing is out of place.* Right, below: *View onto a stoep facing the werf.*

House Gordon,
Plettenberg Bay

Top: *The dramatic look of the outside terrace prefaces the drama of the black-and-white interiors.* Right: *Ebony-stained plantation-style shutters have been used throughout the house. Chairs are slip-covered in simple white cotton. On the floor, a matching Nguni cowhide.*

Could this be one of the smartest beach home makeovers ever? Possibly, given that the decorator was Stephen Falcke. What began life in cottagey chintz is now dramatically different, its guise quasi-Cuban colonial, quasi-pan-African, and heavily dependent for the thoroughness of its look on dark, sometimes ebony-stained, wood (for shutters, furniture, floors, lamp bases) and white (for walls, slipcovers, ranks of crockery, vases and lamp-shades). Black-and-white cowhides on the floor complete the look, giving it its edge. The monochrome scheme would be severe, even daunting, if it wasn't for the comely sofas with large squashy cushions, the flirty slip-covers on the dining chairs, and the softly textured Porthault linen on the beds. The look is simple, but craftily so, and fortified by the fact that it's uncompromising. There's nothing fussy about the furniture; shapes are solid, proportions big, and ornate cornices were replaced with cleaner, simpler lines. Rooms were opened up to allow more leisurely views across the Robberg beach to the ocean directly in front of the house, which like many beach houses is only really used in the summer. This bold decor has panache and style, and it won't easily date.

In the dining room (top left), in the stairwell (bottom left), in the sitting room (right), and in the main bedroom (overleaf), white on black on white. Falcke shows himself a master of maximising impact through his considered approach to application and environment.

Meer Rivier, Klein Karoo

Above, left: A work in progress. Viewed from the front, shutters indicate the need to replace metal windows with wooden sashes. **Above, right:** *In the bathroom stacked reading matter for time out in the Klein Karoo.* **Right:** *View from the stoep.*

Once occupied by sheep and bats, and for years used as a windbreak by wandering springbok, a 19th-century cottage on a mountain slope on the R62 in the Klein Karoo has been brought back to life. It's a rough place, the former shelter of bywoners who eked out what living they could from the surrounding fields, kept cattle and lived in low-ceilinged rooms blackened by woodsmoke. The roof is tin, the walls lime-washed, sun-baked brick, the floor swept and polished cement and dung and the ceilings sugar-washed bamboo. Patched up, its simply furnished, unfussy rooms look out on an uncompromising – but compelling – landscape, blazing hot through summer and freezing in winter. There's no electricity. Water from the nearby stream flows into an outside tank and is heated by gas. All over the Klein Karoo are houses like these, the ideal antidote to softened-up urban living.

Above: *Keeping it simple: a well-swept cement floor, an ancient sugar-washed bamboo ceiling and whitewashed walls are the best setting for plain wooden furniture in the living room. The bateau lit is Mexican and terracotta bowl Spanish.* **Right:** *A no-frills colour scheme works best out in the veld. The black-and-white plaid is 18th-century Scottish, the chair suspended on the wall came from a skip in London, while the busts of Napoleon and Josephine found their way here from the shop at the Louvre in Paris.*

44

Farmhouse, Oranjezicht

Above: *The entrance front with Lion's Head beyond.* **Right:** *In the kitchen thee dining table and benches are washed wood, while the serving table in the hearth has eucalyptus-green legs.*

It takes a master stylist to treat a house as traditional as this Cape Dutch homestead as a blank canvas. Owner Karen Roos has composed her interiors with a curator's eye, recombining disparate elements for style and comfort. The key here is her understanding of colour: you only need look at the fearless experimenting with colour bursts and snatches in French green and raspberry pink. She has, in her own words, 'steered clear of the sacred cows of Cape Dutch vernacular', and refused the restrictions of period decorating. Interiors put together by somebody who knows how to break the rules and get away with it.

Left: *The absence of formal co-ordination in the green library is quite intentional.* Above: *Quiet tones and styling in the living room with linen slipcovers and cushions with strips of pink jacquard trim and knocked-back Gustavian plaid. The bareness and simplicity recall the sober styling of a traditional Dutch interior.*

Beach House, Cape Agulhas

The approach to the house (above left). From the sitting room you can look out to sea across the broad terrace of travertine slabs (above right), while on the other side of the house (right) a sheltered land-facing terrace makes the most of the low, open landscape surrounding it.

A buff of jagged rocks is all that separates this holiday house from the sea. To one side a wild ocean on the Cape coast, to the other fynbos and steep mountain slopes. And while the building has successfully captured the character of its unique setting, nature is never allowed to dominate. The owner's ideas were carried forward by Stefan Antoni Architects, a collaboration that has produced a home where the distinctions between inside and out are blurred. More glass than wall, this house both embraces its magical surroundings and provides a bulwark against them in hostile weather conditions. Although coastal winds of up to 50 knots are not unknown, the house is positioned in such a way that the occupants are never disturbed by storms. Most houses broadcast a sense of arrival as you go inside. Here, though, the approach over a low incline allows you to digest where you are before you actually enter a building which has neither hall nor corridors. Inside, a huge open-plan living space containing kitchen, dining and sitting areas opens onto bedrooms and bathrooms in which large windows slide back, in turn opening up the rooms to sea and sky. And while modernity can be hard to live with – literally – particularly on holiday, this building's natural materials, the lines of the interior construction, as well as the choice of furnishing fabrics are soft, even sensual. They enfold you and invite you to stay.

Above: *In the tactile warmth of the bedroom, a 'Neoz' bed by Philippe Starck with removable bed-head cover of Irish linen.*

Right: *An old Balinese teak dining table and Oscar Tusquets woven wicker chairs separate a comfortable fireside sofa from the kitchen.*

Leadwood Lodge,
KwaZulu-Natal

Cultural references are mixed, nowhere more enigmatically than in this view of the owner's moated study with its serpentine shale walls (top left), the stoep in the dappled shadow of latte (top right), and in the large sitting room with its double-volume stone-clad fireplace (right).

Homes of massive proportions, and this one verges close on 100 metres end to end, seldom feel consolidated. Not here. Leadwood Lodge is alive with spirit of place, and infused with the big-hearted energy of the wild outdoors. That you feel part of, and drawn to, the landscape is thanks to the site and the ground plan, inspired by the safari camp ideal. Architect Bruce Stafford positioned the building in a wide bowl of thorn trees and grassland facing an iconic African view. His bush vernacular of curvy, swooping walls, pitched thatched roofs and epic spaces made of natural but polished materials prompts you to engage emotionally, even sensually. The owner set out to create something out of the ordinary: a spectacular take on gracious African living inspired by the look Cécile and Boyd's design director, Boyd Ferguson, has made his own. 'This was about organic Africa. Curves, exaggerated texture, nothing painted, flat or plain,' says Ferguson. 'In contrast, the decor was about clarity and simplicity'. Bush colours, including straw, white, coral, leaf green, red and tan, were applied to rooms in a single colour signature with tonal and textural high points. 'There is an earthy splendour to this place which comes from the location and scale of the landscape, of course, but also from the proportions, finishes and form of the furnishings. The way they all work together contributes to the robust visual flavour,' Ferguson explains.

Left: *Exterior walls of dry-packed shale echo structures at Great Zimbabwe.* **Above:** *There's an earthy splendour to the scale and textural finishes of this house.*

Decking meets raw bushveld. **Overleaf:** *Beneath the roof, milky white upholstery on chairs and sofas contributes to the feeling of cool as well as cosiness.*

Left: *The main bedroom's four-poster bed tented with a suspended mosquito net.* **Above:** *Open-air dining with all the thrill of the wilds.*

The Post House, Rosebank

Opposite and below: *At the entrance, the choice of motifs is iconic. Above, a mirrored sunburst. Below, feathered headdresses.* Top: *Decorator Nthabi Taukobong is in the vanguard of a new take on African decor.* Overleaf: *The look throughout is uncompromisingly African: colours, textures, patterns.*

Foremost in decorator Nthabi Taukobong's mind is the need to come up with a new South African aesthetic. 'We need to define ourselves and develop an African style. And it needn't be a kitsch take on predictable African designs, like the zig-zag Ndebele patterns,' she says. 'It's about defining the realness of where we come from ... it's not about throwing a Zulu pot onto a table and saying "That's African".' She's right. That kind of interpretation is too literal. It's really the colours and textures of Africa that should inspire, and that's what you see in this living space in Rosebank, Johannesburg, designed for a young 'cosmo-African' couple by Taukobong's Moago Interiors. It's very specific to the quick pace of the locale; it's a no-nonsense, no-frills look with a note of sturdy masculinity. It's also a bold, urban aesthetic that speaks of an unfolding smart new world confident of its heritage.

Garden Cottage,
Parktown North

Above: *The stoep at Garden Cottage has everything on it that an inside sitting room would require.* Opposite: *The design of the house hints at an older Johannesburg vernacular.* Overleaf: *The single large living room is informally divided by an array of seating options. Each area is an island separate from its neighbour but linked by colour themes, similar scale, and so on. Alone, your mood or activity governs where you choose to sit. For parties, there are pockets for different conversations. This is both a private space and an entertainer's one.*

This is the extra house everyone dreams of having. You go there to play house. You don't live there, but go there to swim, or have dinners, have a nap or potter in the garden. And then you go home. In fact this house has an unusual genesis in that decorator Stephen Falcke designed the pool and garden first, then added the house to complement them. It's all quite simple really. There's a potager in front, in a gravelled courtyard, and a long narrow reflective lap pool at the back. In the centre, across the site, the house has a single main room, a tiny kitchen and a bathroom and, facing the pool, a deep, shaded stoep for summer enjoyment. There's a very South African corrugated iron roof, the kind old Johannesburg mining homesteads had, and there are no gutters, 'so that I can enjoy the din and smells of summer thunderstorms and watch the rain splashing off the roof'. If you like to design rooms and enjoy playing with furniture, then study one of Falcke's rooms. His own sitting room here is the perfect place to begin. There are side tables the right height to put your drinks on, and lamps precisely where you need them. Nothing is left to chance. Old linens, Kuba cloths, wrought-iron and teak furniture, hurricane lamps and lacquered boxes litter the place. This is the holiday house in France for the holiday he hadn't time to take, the bush lodge retreat he never gets to. This is a fantasy turned into reality.

Above: *A formal dining area within an informal setting.* **Opposite:** *Comfort zone. The stoep with its sofas, lamps, chairs and coffee tables, has been laid out perfectly as another room.*

Vygekraal, Plettenberg Bay

This quirky beach house and family home outside Plettenberg Bay masquerades as a castle and manipulates the scenery to take unfair advantage of the locale – it looks as if the landscape has been created especially as a backdrop for an improbable castle. The latter is located on a cliff edge amidst the wildflowers of Vygekraal and terraces and balconies perch precariously above vertiginous drops to the rough seas below. The owner has played with elements of gothic fantasy in what she calls her '*folie de grandeur*' and the eclectic decor features brightly coloured fabrics from India and Malabar, antique Dutch chandeliers and African basket work. There's eccentricity, but also a generous, expansive ambience in the oversized sofas and chairs, and family memorabilia. It's a castle that has nothing of the brooding fortress about it and doesn't take itself too seriously.

Above: *This bathroom is the most dramatic gesture of all. From it there are views way out over a wild and rocky coastline.* **Opposite:** *Scattered around the building are various vantage points from which to admire the view. Here the west terrace sunbathing 'pit' and dining area make the most of their setting. Wicker, hammocks and deep cushions are key elements.*

Royal Malewane,
Limpopo Province

Suspended in tree tops on the western border of the Kruger National Park, this luxury game lodge was original-ly a private family lodge for the Biden family. Natural vernacular was the starting point: in lieu of paint, marble dust was mixed into the plaster to create a soft, natural tone that absorbs the changing light, blinds were woven from local reed and soaring 10-metre ceilings clad in thatch all enhance the fantasy of living up a tree. Decorator Ralph Krall worked with owner Liz Biden to mix colonial Dutch and English furniture against the neutral palette. Add to this the improbable luxury of Isfahan carpets in rich red tones, finely embroidered linen from China, Ralph Lauren bedding, African art and prints, antique porcelain, silver and crystal. This is the Victorian safari tradition revived with tongue firmly in cheek. Major pieces of furniture sit happily out in the open under blue skies or the starry Southern Cross; the frisson of pampered domestic comfort in the wilds never palls.

Each suite has its own private relaxation area; it's al fresco living at its finest.

Above: *Getting into a high bed requires the assistance of a set of library steps. From here there are fine views through facing windows out to the bush beyond.* Right: *It's all about space and scale here; both are generous. In the end nothing could be more luxurious.*

Long Barn, Hyde Park

Top: *This single large house has been conceived as a cluster of separate buildings and has the rambling look of a farmstead.* Below: *Decorator Julia Twigg.* Right: *At the entrance a screen of books has been pierced by a door which opens to an enfilade of rooms linked by stone floors.*

The name given to the house was not only literal – a great barn of a house – but literary, recalling Vita Sackville-West and *Portrait of a Marriage*. Unlike Sackville-West, who moved from Long Barn to the grandeur of Sissinghurst, the owner here wanted a simpler and more informal lifestyle. She brought in decorator Julia Twigg to arrange furniture designed by Imrie Loerincz alongside chubby Provençal pots and unlined barley linen curtains to create a deliberately undecorated look. Twigg has no truck with what she calls 'the froufrou of swags and tails' and worked here to create beautifully proportioned and unfussy interiors with Cecil Adams furniture and 18th-century oils in one room, a scarred sheep-shearer's table of pine in another. This is a glamorous farmhouse in urban Parkhurst that happily juxtaposes rough and refined.

Left: *In the drawing room, Imrie Loerincz' richly coloured sofas make a dramatic statement. The spacious room is simply organised and derives its style from generously proportioned furnishings and a robust fireplace.* Above: *An antique sheep-shearer's table in pine dominates the kitchen.*

Tradouw's Hoek, Klein Karoo

At the core of Philip Uys' cottage is a rough shepherd's hut constructed using lovely dry stone walls typical of the tract of Klein Karoo in which he's chosen to live. It stands at the top of a wide, shallow valley which opens dramatically onto one of those magnificent Karoo vistas which go on and on into the distance. And there's nothing here but him and the dam he's building. Once an antique dealer in Pretoria, and now the owner of a country hotel not far away, he decamped, as it were, to this valley for a bit of peace and quiet. There's television and a music system for blasting away the silence, and he can plug in the laptop; but otherwise paraffin lamps light the evenings and cooking is over gas. Uys lives outside on the stoep: there's a desk, a dining table and big armchairs, and there's a fireplace for braais. After dinner you sprawl on the low wide walls encircling the stoep and gaze up at the Milky Way which is nowhere more magnificent than on a black Karoo night.

Above: *Robust and simple, this country cottage has a no-frills style that sits well with the stony landscape all around.* **Opposite:** *The enclosed stoep.*

Above: *In the kitchen the dining table is usually more chopping board and bar than a social centre. Most meals are eaten on the stoep.* **Right:** *The bedroom with rietdak and gumpole ceiling, iron bedstead and kaross is the quiet country bedroom of nostalgic fantasy. Think Story of an African Farm.*

Apartment, Clifton

It's enormously challenging to build on Clifton. Near vertiginous drops from the road to the sea preclude anything but the most dramatic buildings. You have these demanding, 'look-at-me' views of the smart sandy beaches below, the Atlantic with its summer yachts and, if you're lucky, the peaks of the Twelve Apostles towering over everything. This is not a location for timid, down-home types, which is why the owners of this apartment called in Stefan Antoni Architects. Their immediate response was to open up three existing units, transforming them into a vast living area characterised, perhaps uniquely in this stretch of glitzy real estate, by an intelligent sense of design, an eye for quality and the relentless pursuit of perfection. The sense of space is remarkable: imagine you're in a double-volume, well-heeled art gallery in which the spaces simply flow without visual barriers. Everything merges as formal becomes informal, while wraparound views embrace the surroundings. This is a glorious, sensual space which by day is drenched in sunlight and by night takes on an a dramatic sense of cool. It's beachside living at its sleekest.

Above: This beachside apartment embraces the natural grandeur of its surroundings. Opposite: The double-height reception area with its upper gallery looks out to sea.

Above: *The main bedroom is entered off the upstairs sculpture gallery.*

Above, clockwise from top left: *Above the dining table, a shallow barrel vault articulates the ceiling; in the bathroom distinctive panels of sandblasted glass in a seaweed pattern; striking a pose above the ocean; glass balustrading and white marble ensure a light airy stairwell.*

5 Jarvis Street, Green Point

A master of fantasy, Keith Skeel took a wreck at the heart of Cape Town and bravely transformed it into a home that's anything but ordinary. 'I hate ugliness,' he said, and went on to furnish and embellish this old terraced dwelling with an eccentric array of Oriental-style furniture, ancient pewter, old French shop fittings, recycled junk and driftwood, and covered the sitting room armchairs in 19th-century linen sheets. He has an extraordinary eye, and it commands the unexpected to appear utterly normal. Of course the fridge is covered in wallpaper and the courtyard has a waterfall. There isn't much colour about the place though; he prefers the look of wood and adeptly layers different timbers with stone and fabric. Nothing 'goes with' anything. There's nothing safe here. But that's deliberate. Keith loves to live with a little bit of drama.

Top: *The staircase has a Gaudi-inspired handrail fashioned from a dead branching tree trunk picked up in the veld.* Right: *The thickly planted roof garden belies the house's inner city address.*

Above: *The Edwardian-inspired bathroom is of honed marble with a Cape Dutch linen press.* Right: *The walnut dining table is Spanish, bought in Toulouse. Behind that, a server from Manila flanked by two bishop's chairs and above that on the wall a Dutch plate rack stacked with Bristol blue glass and pewter.*

Left: *Far end of the bedroom framed by 19th-century fruitwood doors hiding a dressing room.*

Above: *Detail of a confidently assembled collection of African carved drums, tree trunks and artefacts.*

Above: *Courtyard grotto with waterfall, palms, Scottish ceramic chair and Victorian cast-iron table.* Right: *The French bookcase in the living room holds curios and artefacts. The tree-trunk table bases were bought in Manila and repolished in England.*

Kurland Hotel, The Crags

Above: *At the heart of estate, the polo pavilion designed by Martin Rattray* Above right: *Diane Behr (right) and her sister Glenda Lederle in the flower room, presided over the transformation of Kurland from dilapidated homestead to hotel* Right: *There's a great sense of femininity at Kurland, manifest in pretty table arrangements and lashings of flowers from the gardens.*

This must be one of the most charming houses in South Africa. With her sister Glenda Lederle, Di Behr was set the task of retrieving what she could of the old farmhouse at the heart of an estate that once stretched from The Crags to Robberg at Plettenberg Bay. The existing house was old but simply built. Over the last 60 years buildings had been expanded by the Behrs to accommodate friends and family, and a building style evolved to incorporate distinctive Cape Dutch-style gables, white-washed walls and charcoal corrugated-iron roofing. Now a hotel, and the Plettenberg Bay hub for local and international polo players, the results are delightful. Rooms were opened up, a gallery created, yellowwood floors waxed and polished, and handmade clay tiles laid in the entrance. Farm cottages under century-old trees were transformed into lofty bedrooms with spacious, glamorous bathrooms. The old verandah acquired a reed ceiling and a red-polished floor. Family antiques include Cape stinkwood armoires, chests and tables, as well as finds from Clignancourt in Paris and further afield. The gallery was painted Wedgwood blue and chinoiserie-patterned curtains were hung from bamboo poles. Bedrooms were inspired in part by Jacques Garçia's stylish rooms at the Hotel Costes in Paris. A refinement of taste European, American or African? Doesn't really matter. Sensational interiors easily credible by any international standard.

Above: *Each of the bedrooms (there are 12 suites) is a sophisticated layering of fabrics and antique or modern furniture – antique from French* marches aux puces, *modern from Johannesburg or Cape Town. No need is left unaccounted for, no surface left bare.* **Right:** *The library is a comfort zone more for cocooning than reading.*

A small private pool has a pretty Cape Dutch-style gable. **Right:** *The stoep, an increasingly important living space in South African homes. Neither inside nor out, they proclaim an easy lifestyle. It's the drawing room come to Africa.*

Cheviot Place, Green Point

Above: *Important objects displayed with bric-a-brac mark this as the house of an eclectic collector.*
Right: *A narrow hall was opened up letting in light from the dining room.*

Craig Kaplan's Edwardian house at Cheviot Place isn't a decorated sort of house, and no attempt has been made to soften the lines with upholstery or carpets. Formerly a poky dwelling at the end of a terrace, it was opened up by Kaplan to let in the light and free the constricted space in the period rooms. Both upstairs and down, suites of rooms are now only separated from one another by a fireplace, the walls on either side of the chimney breast having been removed to allow views into the spaces on either side and beyond. This is the house of a man who can't say no. Years of booty hunting in salesrooms and antique shops up and down the country have filled the rooms with paintings, sculpture, furniture and glass in a range of styles and from different periods, from the 18th century to the 1970s. This house, then, is unabashedly a storeroom for disparate beautiful things that have been collected simply because they appealed to Kaplan over the years. Some finds are more worthy than others. Many aren't supposed to work together. That they do is a happy coincidence.

Above: *Mix and match: in the bedroom, partially carved from a corridor, a painting by Anton Karstel hangs above the bed. At its foot, a 1930s French shagreen desk.*

Right: *Here and there are whimsical side-shows of disparate collected objects.*

Above: *The living room's eclectic array of furniture includes 1950s Danish recliners, 1970s armchairs, an Edwardian club chair and a Biedemeier table. Above the sofa,* Jo'burg Man *by Arlene Amaler-Raviv.* Right: *The bathroom, once a small back room, now has pride of place in a converted bedroom. On white-painted floor boards, an Nguni cowhide.*

Villa 16, Sandhurst Estate

Above: *The private deck off the main bedroom looks out over Sandton.* Right: *Beyond Tony Nkotsi's painting facing the bar, is the living room with, above the fireplace, a work by Claire Gavronsky.*

This house contains the most astonishing collection of art and artefacts. In fact Villa 16 in Sandhurst is a showcase for the work of South African craftsmen, put together by a globetrotting businessman who combines a sense of fun with a serious passion for collecting. Paris-based designer Serge Robin and South African architect Peter Hoffe were given creative carte blanche to create something exceptional and they did, the former designing everything from sofas and tables to curtains and carpeting, most of it manufactured in South Africa. 'The owner,' says writer Josef Talotta, 'is more than enthusiastic about South African craftsmanship,' comparing it to the best in the world. The house also showcases the work of South African artists like André Naude, Tony Nkotsi, Simon Stone and Louis van Heerden.

Above: *An expandable dining table seats up to 14 people; dining chairs are a combination of French originals and locally made reproductions. Handblown Venetian glass chandelier, art by Louis van Heerden.* Right: *A masculine aesthetic in the living room mixes stone, leather, wood and chrome.*

Knoetzie, Knysna

As a castle it could be located anywhere, on any wild misty coastline from Eastern Europe to Scotland to South Africa's Knysna. A Scottish emigrant at the turn of the last century thought the undeveloped Knysna coast reminded him of the Hebrides and bought property there. He built a garden shed of quarried stone to amuse his wife and, on a whim, added parapets. He went on to build two castle follies. Current owner Ineke Henderson of Pezula Interiors in Plettenberg Bay chose a restrained palette to emphasise the stonework and natural drama of seas, sky and sand. 'I don't "decorate",' says Henderson. 'With a folly on this scale, you either go over the top or pare it all down. I preferred to underdress in greys, blues, creams. It's impossibly romantic, so I needed strong pieces that felt right in such a gothic setting. Knoetzie also had to work as a comfortable family beach house.'

Above: *The 'battlements' provide a useful parapet over which to take in the view.* Right: *A narrow, defunct outside passage was glassed over to expand the sitting room. Kudu horns, baskets and colours of the veld give context.*

116

Above, clockwise from top left: *Alfresco terrace dining; a private terrace with recliners in crisp white cottons and indigo prints opens from a tower bedroom; the dining room occupies the principal floor of the 'keep'; castellated mansion, or seaside folly? Both, actually.* Right: *The tower stair inadvertently borrows its masculine prowess from Lutyens' Castle Drogo.*

Silverhurst, Constantia

Interior designer Boyd Ferguson is as much a master of constructing 'social' arrangements of furniture as he is at arranging armies of disparate objects on tabletops and other surfaces. He's big on scale, has a deft hand with colour and texture, and creates rooms which are contemporary but with a recognisably traditional provenance. This large Constantia house in the Cape has it all in heaps and, while its look strikes an undeniably luxurious note, it is in the end a functional dwelling perfect for a busy couple with two children. It's a cosily sophisticated place that relies on the impeccable taste of its decorator to clear the hurdles which might otherwise render it simply another suburban home in a neighbourhood of others like it. The glossy black-and-white marble floor is an unexpected keynote, as are the gallery-like arrangements of pictures on the walls. Elements such as the Chinese screens in sepia, umber and blue tones flanking the high double doors – which in turn lead into a drawing room dominated by low, armless sofas covered in wheat-blond bouclé – give it the quiet grace you might expect to find in the salon of a gifted couturier who doesn't need to shout about his talents.

Previous top: *A cool green and white colour scheme on the stoep has been inspired by Beatonesque island villas.* **Previous right:** *From the drawing room, a view through to the dining room.* **Above:** *In the hall an Adams-style console.* **Right:** *An art collection lines the walls of the hall.*

Onrust, Calitzdorp

Artist-potter Hylton Nel moved to Calitzdorp in the Klein Karoo from Bethulie almost two years ago. He bought a farmstead originally built in the 1830s and it had all the things Karoo-lovers fall for when house-hunting there – a tin roof, deep stoep, sash windows, old glass. 'It just seemed so perfect,' says Nel. The oldest walls were built of cob, clay mixed with straw. In the 1880s clay bricks were used and, during the 1970s renovations, concrete bricks. He shows an artist's appreciation of raw materials and replastered the house and enlarged the stoep. His house is filled with art; but where does art end and domestic use begin, you wonder, as you notice his not-inexpensive ceramics covering every surface? In fact he's surrounded himself with them, his own and the work of others, as an inspiration and a reference. Art dealer Michael Stevenson has described Nel's work as 'modest, domestic and humane' which is why pots and plates are at home in these interiors, stacked on shelves and used for eating off and holding bunches of flowers. 'I try to make objects as real as I can,' says Nel, which is why they sit well alongside the bits of African sculpture, iron-age tools, baskets, miscellaneous books, European porcelain and droves of other oddments inherited, collected or simply found. 'I love all kinds of *things*,' he says.

Above: *Examples of Hylton Nel's erotic, irreverent and whimsical plates, many exhibited previously at Michael Stevenson's Contemporary Art Gallery.* **Opposite:** *View through the living room into the study. An oaken mule chest with Imari jar on the right; white Ming porcelain on the left; at the back a Georgian cupboard with 'mostly old English ceramics'.*

Karooltjie, Barrydale

This extraordinary little house began life on the back of an envelope as a drawing of three petals of a flower. At the heart of a vineyard, amongst some trees by a river, owners Gerald and Carol Phillips wanted something 'organic' and so, matching the project to an architect, came up with Etienne Bruwer of Greenhaus Architects, a disciple of Austrian thinker Rudolf Steiner and influenced by modern organic architects such as Gaudi and Aalto. On plan it is essentially three spaces – a main bedroom, a main living area, and a guest bedroom – packed together loosely behind a remarkable dry-packed stone perimeter wall. Owners and architect wanted to experiment with different types of masonry. There's plenty of slate in the neighbourhood, and an interesting tradition of local use because local craftsmen had been taught how to better their skills by Italian masons set to work on the restoration of nearby Tradouw Pass during World War II. There's dry-packed stone on the outside of Karooltjie, cut stone within and the mortar is lime mixed with clay. Leftover stone was used to cover the roof. In a welcome development, this project has rekindled the art of using natural stone for building in the region.

Left: *This deep stoep, which faces a shady wooded space, allows a gradual transition of light and temperature from the outside to the interior. It's Karooltjie at its most open. Everywhere else, windows are few.* **Above:** *Looking down from the roof to the outside shower and the formal rill in the little rose garden beyond...*

Parkside, Oranjezicht

Ralph Krall lives in a colonial villa on the edge of an old pine-filled public park in Cape Town. Its interior is a masterpiece of layering: furniture might line, and jut out from, the walls, but on it are carefully massed objects for depth and statuettes for height, while behind these are little framed pictures that lean against larger paintings hanging right at the back, on the wall. 'This is my forte,' says this decorator, who likens what he does to the planting of borders in the garden. 'Things grow in front of other things and you decide what goes where through massing, colour and shape.' Layering therefore is key. Above all though, his houses are comfortable. 'I work with my gut-feel. Comfort first. Then quality (of fabric and furnishings), and then the look.' He should add colour in there somewhere too: 'If you're afraid of it, you've had it.' And so Parkside is filled with the rich and opulent tones of painted wood, various fabrics upholstering the furniture and lining the walls, paintings, Oriental ceramics and carpets. Colour is not explored much in South African interiors. Here it brings the interiors to life, passionately.

Above: *The ponderous entrance façades of the villa recall an architectural style once common in turn-of-the-century Cape Town.* **Right:** *Decorator Ralph Krall.*

Above: *This aqua bathroom is the only remnant of the previous owners' follies. Solid wood North African mannequins stand dazed beneath the deep aqua ceiling.* Opposite: *Opulent, dramatic, irreverent: the dining room from the hall.*

Left: *A bedroom beneath the library stacks painted in Japanese colours is revealed through arches leading from the sitting room.*

Above: *This bedroom with its fabric-clad walls, rich colours and ornate Indian bed, is all about comfort.*

Villa Libert, St James

It's one thing to appreciate arched and porticoed Spanish Colonial combined with Cape Dutch vernacular on the False Bay coastline, all in dressed stone on a massive scale. It's another thing to be able to make such a house livable and comfortable for the 21st century. Here decorator Keith Skeel has taken a few liberties and opened up small dark rooms to let in the air and take absolute advantage of one of the best views over False Bay. This handsome house has been made to work as a contemporary seaside home with large period furniture and lots of space for easy living. The main frontage houses, at ground level, a panelled sitting room and dining room in their original positions, while above are two large bedrooms, each with an enormous bathroom. Bathing in Edwardian times was obviously not an upfront function of lifestyle; Skeel put paid to that 'behind-closed-doors' notion, opening up views to the ocean from the tub and providing volumes of space for towels and seats and splashing water. At the back of the house a warren of little rooms survives to provide guest bedrooms, offices, kitchens and storage. Villa Libert may look huge, but it is manageable at last, mixing comfort with domesticity.

Above: *In the main bedroom, which opens onto a private stoep facing the sea, an early Cape Dutch armoire and a carved four-poster bed are both punchy and bold.*

Right: *Panelling, both unadorned and mirrored, characterises the formal dining room, nicknamed 'Versailles'.*

Left: *Porticoed seating area with antique wicker and sea breezes.* **Above:** *At the entrance, a columned porch hints at past visits to Cordoba in Spain.*

Mudief, Johannesburg

Above: *African and Arabic influences combine in a contemporary house the colour of mud.* Right: *The artist and collector Karel Nel with examples from his collection of artefacts.*

'Africa is never opulent,' says artist Karel Nel. 'Space is the great luxury.' His home in Johannesburg's northern suburbs has spare, gallery-like proportions. It is very much a work-in-progress ('to be built in phases'), designed by English architect Dexter Moren. The house is built 'in' to its site, and not 'on' it so it's visually integrated into the landscape and not dominating – despite its scale. A series of massive sculptural mounds dot the garden, each home to a different variety of sword-shaped or spiky indigenous plants. Graphic shapes and tactile textures are repeated throughout the home, allowing Nel's valuable collections of African artefacts and specific architectural elements – like the ancient Zanzibar doors – to come to the visual fore. A work of art in the making.

Left: *Furniture by Le Corbusier and Mies van der Rohe alongside 18th-century Chinese seats and pieces from Cameroon and Micronesia. The grass screen is Tutsi, from Rwanda, and the two background panels are from Nel's* Elegies to the Forest *on baobab fibre collected in Madagascar.* **Above:** *A Baule mask (from the Emile Storrer collection in Zürich) overlooks a Le Corbusier lounger adjacent to a lounger from Upper Volta.*

Singita Sweni, Mpumalanga

The bush aesthetic doesn't come any wittier. Singita Sweni, like its near neighbour Lebombo, was designed to

'tread the earth lightly', the plan being that in 20 years time it should be possible to remove the buildings and

leave no trace of their existence. So they skim the surface of the ground, light airy structures that designer Boyd

Ferguson and architect Andrew Makin have conjured out of leather, canvas, wood and glass on rhyolite cliffs

overlooking the confluence of the Nwanetsi and Sweni Rivers on a 16 000-hectare concession in the Kruger

National Park. In conception, they utterly explode the old paradigms of those colonial-type lodges that populate

the bush. There's no campaign furniture here, or anything remotely reminiscent of Happy Valley. Singita Sweni has

a chic about it that deconstructs the tired old look, going instead for a surprising aesthetic that features, for

example, Landrover seating canvas upholstery for the sofas. It breaks new ground for the bush aesthetic by

taking all we love about safari chic – leather, canvas, khaki – and transforming it into nesting and comfort cues.

Previous: *The main sitting room. As the lodge is settled in a leafy canopy of trees, Ferguson used dark polished woods, chocolate and umber shades of leather and suede, and Landrover canvas ripcord for the sofas.* Left: *A view from the bathroom to the outside shower.* **Above:** *A bedroom with rustic canopy and tie-dye mohair throw on the bed.*

Below: *Wooden pots at the entrance.*
Right: *Viewing platform, furniture of woven abaca leaf and leather.*

Birkenhead House, Hermanus

There are few smarter places from which to view the rare Southern Right whale than the terrace of Birkenhead House, looking out over Walker Bay from the top of a cliff. This is a hotel, a landmark in fact, that evokes pleasurably nostalgic memories of long family lunches and afternoon teas with granny. In its first incarnation Birkenhead House was a family hotel which, after a fire, was demolished. Its current owner, Liz Biden, bought the property and built a clifftop holiday home that recently metamorphosed into a hotel whose trademark is a style of decor best described as restrained opulence. Biden and decorator Ralph Krall accessorised 11 studio suites, some featuring sunken Roman-style baths, with Art Deco lamps and chandeliers, taffeta curtains, monogrammed Ralph Lauren throws and antique Chinese embroidered linen. There's a very sensual tone about the place; perhaps it's the shagreen-covered furniture in some rooms and the mirrored pieces in others. Or could it be the virginal white of the sitting room furniture, or the lavish female nudes hanging on the walls?

Left: *The reception areas may be smart, but they're always comfortable.* **Above, clockwise from top left:** *Ostrich feather lamp shades and paintings by local artists; luxuriously appointed marble bathroom; everywhere the attention to detail evokes a private residence; Walker Bay from the second pool.*

Newlands Farm, Plettenberg Bay

At the foot of Prince Alfred's Pass, the old stone homestead and barn on the farm Newlands have been transformed into a home used like a stage set that's dressed and undressed as the play progresses. One summer, the sitting room was all stripes; now it's a sort of anteroom to a new sitting room outside on a covered stoep and the stripes have been banished in favour of red velvet or leather upholstery. What was the drawing room is now the library and the main bathroom is now the bedroom, although bath and loo still occupy their old locations. The dining room is now a cinema, soon to become a bedroom, but that's only after the garden vanishes under a monumental lake currently being dug for the roaming game which populate the farm. It's all a moveable feast, and its owner, Gail Behr, has fun conjuring up surprises. Newlands gives new meaning to informal, ad hoc living. Twenty-five people coming for dinner? 'Oh, we'll knock up another table to hold the overflow.' There are serious discussions in the kitchen at the bleached and scrubbed table. There's a riotous stand-off of dogs and smokers in the courtyard. Other guests are catching up in the library. This is a stage set by a pro.

Previous: *Dining room and kitchen merge as the predominant social centre.* **Above:** *In the old barn, the bedroom is dominated by an elderly leaden bath tub.*

Left: *The stoep, formerly the herb garden, has a heated floor.*

Noordhoek Villa, Noordhoek

Left: *Ancient Pompeii may have been in Antony Little's mind when he designed his new summer villa, but it was Herbert Baker's mansion at Noordhoek for Sir Drummond Chaplin that provided the model for its look.* Right: *In the cloakroom a large cabinet drew inspiration from a Roman triumphal arch.*

Antony Little's villa at Noordhoek outside Cape Town is intended for use during summer only. Although it's been designed in the ancient Pompeiian manner, built around a central courtyard, there are no internal corridors. Instead all the rooms open onto a wide, cool stoep, lined with a row of double Tuscan columns, which wraps around the house on its rusticated sandstone basement. Noordhoek Villa's proportions and details are a reference to nearby Noordhoek Manor, which Sir Herbert Baker designed from India where he was collaborating with Lutyens on the new capital at Delhi. Familiar with this Baker *tour de force*, Little distilled from its design certain classic elements and nowhere is this better illustrated than in the magnificence of its siting. To the north it faces towering mountains and to the south it overlooks, in the immediate foreground, a huge swimming pool and beyond that two oceans as they march on towards Cape Point in the far distance. Inside, all the furniture and most of the fittings were made in Cape Town by artisans working to scale-drawings supplied by Little himself, design director and co-founder of Osborne & Little. It's a masterpiece of bespoke accessorising and there's almost certainly nothing else like it anywhere in the country.

PRIVATE COLLECTIONS
ARCHITECTURAL PIECES FURNITURE AND DECORATIVE ELEMENTS

Clockwise from top left: *In the bathrooms the Roman theme continues with contrasting marble layers on the walls; study curtains by Angela Swain suspended from bronze caracal heads by Donald Greig; in the drawing room a backgammon table designed by Little has ogee Ottoman supports; bedrooms are opulent with Osborne & Little fabrics.* **Opposite:** *At the heart of the house an outdoor dining room whose tented ceiling acts as a windbreak.* **Overleaf:** *The drawing room, with Hicks' wrought-iron cobras above the pedimented Tuscan fireplace.*

Whaledance, Kommetjie

Locale was the starting point here. On the beach at Kommetjie, the house was sited on an adjacent estuary teeming with abundant birdlife. And as the house was being built, no fewer than 17 whales were spotted in the bay. So owner Sheila Boardman named the house 'Whaledance' and painted the facade a weathered grey, so that the structure would merge into the coastline. Inside and out the colours borrow their references from sea and mountain, sky and sand. The sitting room is furnished with easy rattan chairs and greys, blues and whites predominate. There are American shutters instead of curtains and the rooms are lined with simple tongue-and-groove strips – in contrast to the 18th-century panelling surrounding the fireplace. It's undeniable stylish, but at the end of the day this is a simple, unfussy beach house that makes the most of its fabulous setting.

Above: *The bedroom has an other-worldly atmosphere appropriate for a holiday house removed from the ordinariness of daily life.* **Right:** *Both bedroom and bathroom are in the loft.*

Forest Hall, The Crags

This secluded, gabled homestead in the forests between Plettenberg Bay and the Tsitsikamma Mountains was not an easy place to revive. Originally built by English immigrant William Newdigate in 1862 as an *aide-mémoire* to his aristocratic antecedents back in England, Forest Hall in its heyday hosted Victorian luminaries like Bishop Grey and Thomas Bains. It was built as an English manor house but, standing in a breach in the cliffs way above the wild African coastline, surrounded by ancient indigenous forest, the genteel landscapes of home seemed increasingly alien and out of place. Gradually the forest took over again and although Newdigate's descendants continued to own the property until well into the 1990s, it was on a rapidly diminishing scale. In 2002, a new and flamboyant owner restored the spacious interiors with their yellowwood ceilings and stinkwood doors and mantels over the huge fireplaces. What had been a gloomy period homestead, empty for most of the 20th century, was given a spare, masculine look in which such things as the 30-seater yellowwood dining table, built specially by local carpenter Marty Reddering, look very much at home. In a final over-the-top gesture by the new owner, a fantasy mural by Carl Maritz depicting the primeval landscape as it might have looked about 10 000 years ago was commissioned by the owner to cover an entire wall in the double-volume entrance hall.

Above: *Incongruously, this English-style house faces a wild African coastline.*
Right: *Big, solid, masculine: this massive table in the dining room identifies the essential look of this large country house deep in the forest.*

Above: *A large gloomy entrance is enriched by a mythic landscape mural showing the locale as it might have looked in prehistoric times.* Right: *On the top floor a freestanding bath occupies one corner of a bedroom.* Overleaf: *The morning room opens onto lawns and the Tsitsikamma Mountains.*